WHAT'S SMALLER THAN A PYGMY SHREW?

Robert E. Wells

Albert Whitman & Company
Morton Grove, Illinois

For my son Jeffrey Robert Wells
and to the memory of his grandfather Ernest Amos Wells,
whom he never knew but would have liked.

Also by Robert E. Wells
Is a Blue Whale the Biggest Thing There Is?
How Do You Lift A Lion?
What's Faster Than a Speeding Cheetah?

Library of Congress Cataloging-in-Publication Data

Wells, Robert E.
What's smaller than a pygmy shrew? / Robert E. Wells.
p. cm.
ISBN 0-8075-8837-7 (hardcover)
ISBN 0-8075-8838-5 (paperback)
1. Nuclear size (Physics)—Juvenile literature. 2. Atoms—
Juvenile literature. 3. Body size—Juvenile literature. 4. Size
perception—Juvenile literature.   [1. Atoms. 2. Size.] I. Title.
QC793.3.N83W45   1995   94-27150
539'.1—dc20   CIP
                                                             AC

Hand-lettering by Robert E. Wells.
The illustration media are pen and acrylic.
Design by Susan B. Cohn.

How small would you say that *small* really is? Is something you can hold in your hand, like a blueberry, small? How about a grain of sand?

Yes, it's true we could call those things small. But in this book, you'll find much, MUCH smaller things—things you cannot ordinarily see.

Unless, of course, you look through a MICROSCOPE.

An ordinary (optical) microscope bends light rays in a way that makes objects appear larger than they really are. With this you can see things you may not have known existed. You can discover, for example, that many tiny creatures live inside a single water drop. But did you know that there is a world of things too small to be seen with an ordinary microscope? To see these things, you need to use a much more powerful instrument—an electron microscope, which uses electrons rather than light rays to scan images. This is the kind that many scientists use.

The world of the Very Small is almost unbelievably tiny, and hard to imagine. But it's quite real. In fact, it's just as real as a blueberry.

Everyone knows you can stretch your mind by thinking big. Do you suppose it's also possible to stretch your mind by thinking small?

This is a PYGMY SHREW. From the end of her nose, to the tip of her tail, she's only 3 inches long.

If you were a pygmy shrew, you'd feel mighty small. Even some TOADSTOOLS would be taller than you!

Compared to an elephant, the largest land mammal, she looks very small indeed.

But pygmy shrew, you're not so small.

Not compared to a LADYBUG.

Ladybugs are a kind of beetle, and beetles are just one of the many kinds of insects.

Pygmy shrews are insect eaters, but they prefer to leave ladybugs alone. They know that ladybugs have a bitter taste!

Not compared to the tiny creatures that live in those water drops on your leaf boat!

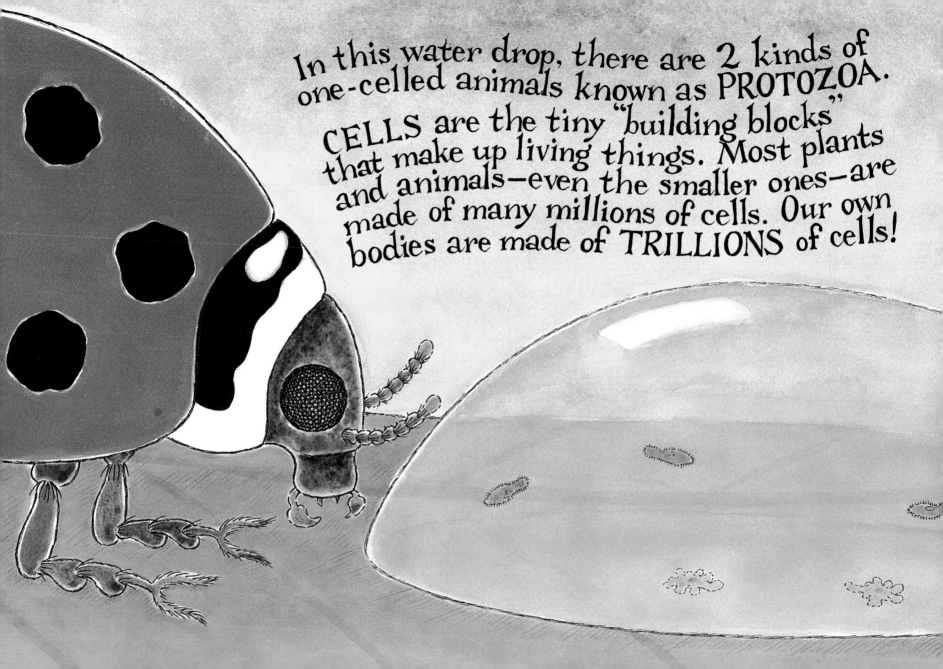

In this water drop, there are 2 kinds of one-celled animals known as PROTOZOA.

CELLS are the tiny "building blocks" that make up living things. Most plants and animals—even the smaller ones—are made of many millions of cells. Our own bodies are made of TRILLIONS of cells!

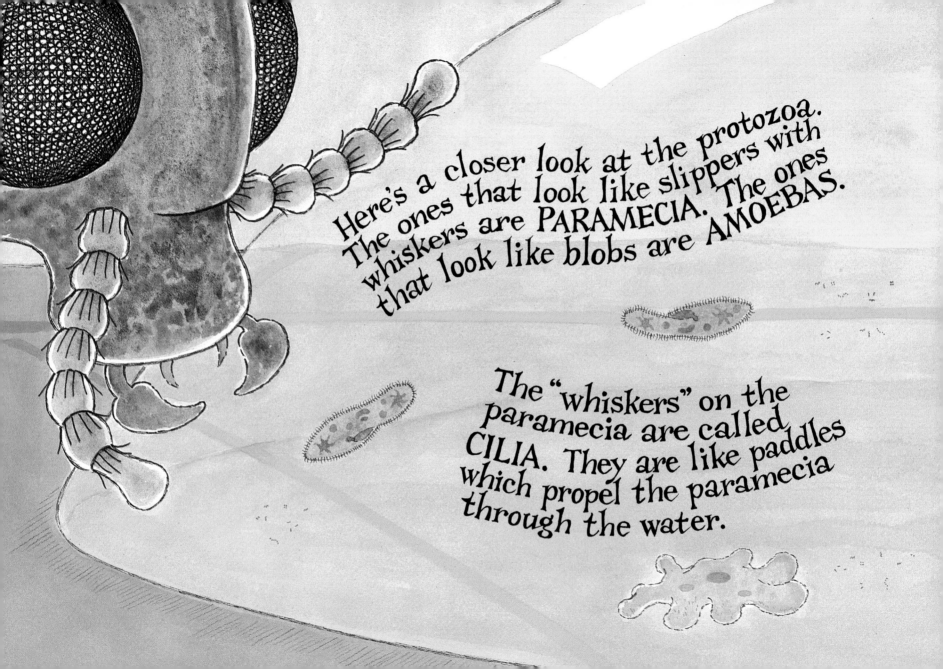

Here's a closer look at the protozoa. The ones that look like slippers with whiskers are PARAMECIA. The ones that look like blobs are AMOEBAS.

The "whiskers" on the paramecia are called CILIA. They are like paddles which propel the paramecia through the water.

An amoeba moves slowly about by pushing out a part of its body, then flowing into that extended part.

Because of this, amoebas are always changing shape!

Paramecia and amoebas are so small that you can barely see them without a microscope.

But did you know that even SMALLER things live inside this drop of water?

Yes, a tiny paramecium would be like a **GIANT SEA MONSTER** compared to **BACTERIA!**

There are many kinds of bacteria. Some cause disease, but most are harmless to people. In fact, many are useful to us because they live inside our bodies and help digest our food.

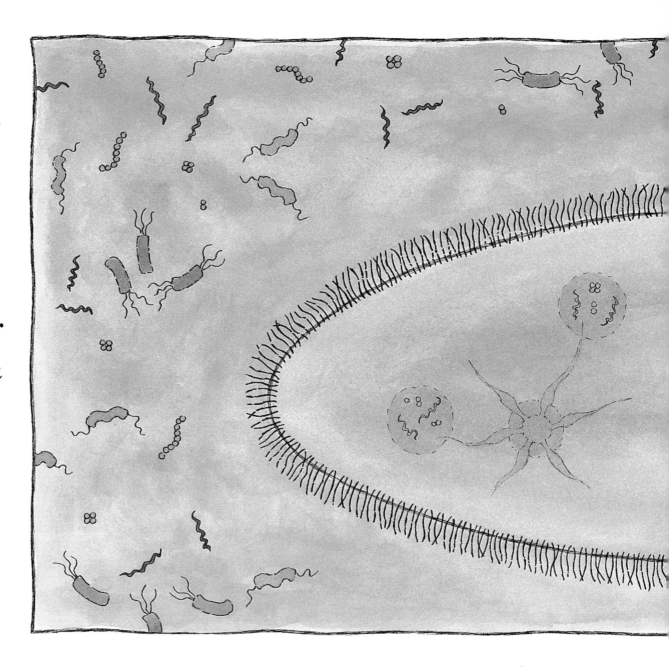

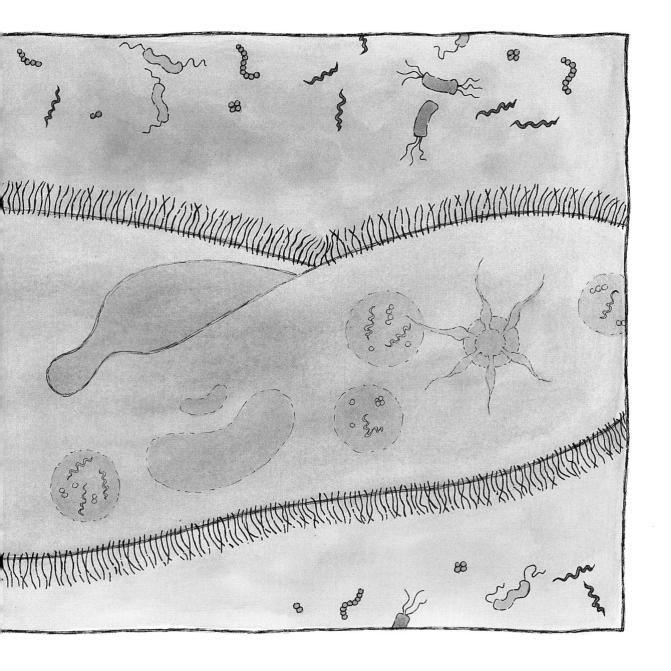

Like protozoa, bacteria are made up of just one cell—but a bacterium cell is smaller and simpler.

Most bacteria are so small that thousands of them could fit on the dot of an *i*.

But even bacteria are made of smaller things called MOLECULES!

Wait! Not so fast!

Before we look at molecules, you have to realize how **INCREDIBLY, ASTONISHINGLY TINY** they really are!

If we took just one part of this bacterium ---->

and made it **THIS SIZE,**

a molecule inside it would still be just a speck!

Living cells—and most of the other things in our world—are made of molecules.

There are many kinds of molecules, and some are much bigger than others. To see even the biggest ones, scientists must use a very powerful, special kind of microscope.

Since all living things contain water, a WATER MOLECULE—the very tiniest particle of water—is one of the many kinds of molecules we would find in this bacterium.

If we picked out just ONE water molecule,

and made
it BIGGER,
it might
look something like THIS.

A water molecule is one of the smallest molecules. It's so tiny that even in this microscopic bacterium, there would be many thousands of them!

But what are those 3 round things that make up the water molecule?

They're
ATOMS!
ALL
molecules
are
made
of
atoms!

There are about 100
kinds of atoms, and they
combine in different ways
to make molecules.

When 2 HYDROGEN atoms combine
with a larger OXYGEN atom, they
make a water molecule like this.

But even those tiny
atoms are made up
of smaller things!

Tiny particles called ELECTRONS whirl around within the atom at about the speed of light, so they would appear as a blur, like a spinning fan blade. Electrons form the cloudy "shells" of the atoms.

The "dot" in the center is the NUCLEUS, shown much bigger than it would really be.

.

Like our universe, atoms are mostly empty space. If an atom were the size of a house, its nucleus would be tinier than a grain of sand!

Here's a closer look at the nucleus of the oxygen atom. Now we can see it's made of even tinier particles. They're called PROTONS and NEUTRONS.

The number of protons determines the kind of atom.

The nucleus of an oxygen atom has 8 protons. It also has 8 neutrons. Neutrons help bond an atom's nucleus together.

Protons and neutrons are made of still tinier particles called QUARKS, with 3 quarks making up each proton and neutron.

Quarks are so amazingly tiny that scientists cannot measure their exact size. But with special machines, they can figure out their weight.

Is a quark, then, the LIGHTEST particle there is?

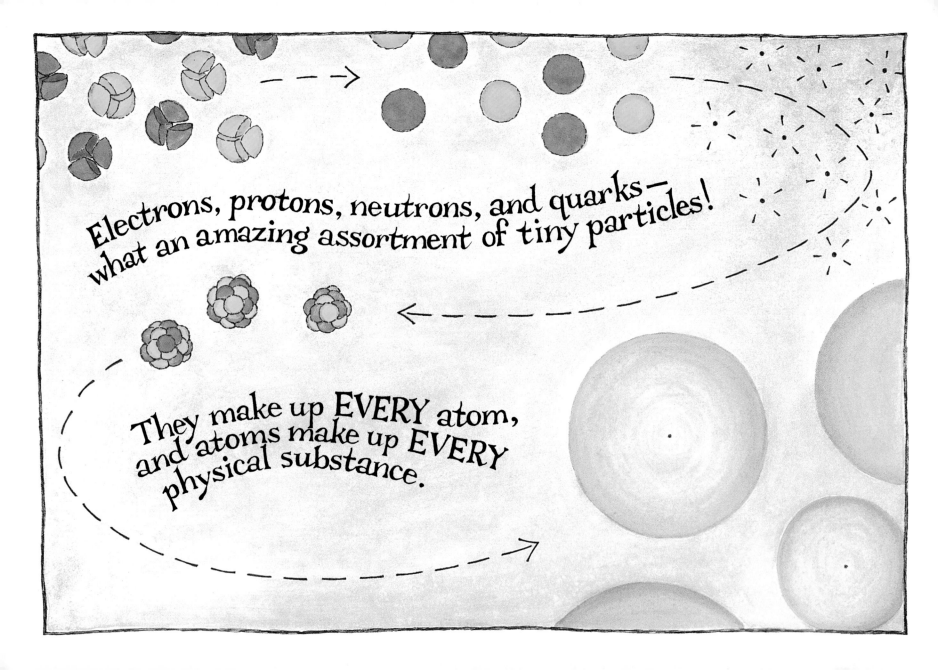

Electrons, protons, neutrons, and quarks— what an amazing assortment of tiny particles!

They make up EVERY atom, and atoms make up EVERY physical substance.

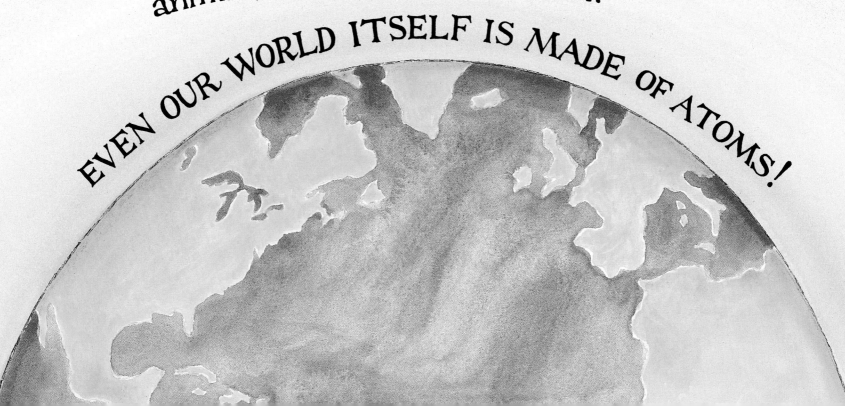

EVERYTHING THAT PEOPLE MAKE is made of atoms. Every car and every clock. Every sink and every shoe. Every boat and every ball.

EVERYTHING IN NATURE is made of atoms. Every grain of sand and every drop of water. Every tree and every flower. Every person, animal, meadow, and mountain.

EVEN OUR WORLD ITSELF IS MADE OF ATOMS!

So is every planet and every star, every comet and every asteroid, every moon and every meteor. In fact, EVERY PHYSICAL THING IN THE UNIVERSE IS

MADE OF ATOMS. TRILLIONS and MORE TRILLIONS and COUNTLESS MORE TRILLIONS OF ATOMS!

How many atoms do you suppose it took to make YOU, pygmy shrew?

A Very Small Glossary

atom composed of electrons, neutrons, and protons, an atom is the smallest unit that makes up a substance. In the 1980s a special microscope was designed that allowed scientists to see atoms for the very first time.

bacteria made up of only one cell, bacteria are among the smallest living things, and they exist almost everywhere on earth. Most bacteria are barely big enough to be seen with an optical microscope. But they are very important to all other living things. They manufacture some of the vitamins and nutrients that plants and animals need. Without bacteria, all other life on earth would soon cease!

cell the smallest living unit of all animals and plants. Cells have the ability to reproduce themselves by dividing in two, and they come in many different shapes and sizes. Most cells are too small to be seen without an optical microscope.

electron a particle within an atom that whirls around the atom's nucleus at nearly the speed of light. An electron is thought to be an elementary particle, which is a particle that is not made up of anything smaller.

molecule made up of atoms, a molecule is the smallest unit of a substance that has all the characteristics of the substance. A molecule can be made of one atom or thousands of atoms.

neutron a particle within an atom that combines with the proton to make up the atom's nucleus. Neutrons help to hold the nucleus together.

nucleus the part at the center of an atom, made up of protons and neutrons.

proton a particle within an atom that combines with the neutron to make up the atom's nucleus. The number of protons determines the kind of atom.

protozoa one-celled animal-like creatures that can be found in salt water, fresh water, soil, plants, and animals. Many protozoa cause disease in humans, but some live in our bodies peacefully.

pygmy shrew an animal so small it can weigh as little as a U.S. penny. It eats mostly insects and worms. Pygmy shrews live in fields, woodlands, gardens, and marshes in both the Eastern and Western hemispheres, including many areas of North America.

quarks tiny particles that make up the neutrons and protons in the nuclei of atoms. Quarks are thought to be elementary particles. Both electrons and quarks have sizes which are too small to measure, but their weights can be calculated.